TRANSCRIPTIONS
TENOR SAXOPHONE

Featuring Note-for-Note
Transcriptions from
A Love Supreme

John Coltrane

Acknowledgement • Resolution • Pursuance / Psalm

ISBN 978-0-634-03887-7

HAL•LEONARD®
CORPORATION

7777 W. BLUEMOUND RD. P.O. BOX 13819 MILWAUKEE, WI 53213

Visit Hal Leonard Online at
www.halleonard.com

Contents

4   Acknowledgement (Part I)

9   Resolution (Part II)

14   Pursuance (Part III)

20   Psalm (Part IV)

Acknowledgement

(Part I)

By John Coltrane

decresc.

52

8

Resolution
(Part II)
By John Coltrane

Piano Solo

92

N.C.(Fm)

Pursuance

(Part III)

By John Coltrane

16

Psalm

(Part IV)
By John Coltrane

ARTIST TRANSCRIPTIONS®

Artist Transcriptions are authentic, note-for-note transcriptions of today's hottest artists in jazz, pop and rock. These outstanding, accurate arrangements are in an easy-to-read format which includes all essential lines. Artist Transcriptions can be used to perform, sequence or for reference.

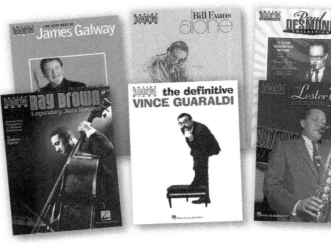

FLUTE

00672379	Eric Dolphy Collection	$19.95
00672582	The Very Best of James Galway	$19.99
00672372	James Moody Collection – Sax and Flute	$19.95

GUITAR & BASS

00660113	Guitar Style of George Benson	$19.99
00672573	Ray Brown – Legendary Jazz Bassist	$22.99
00672331	Ron Carter Collection	$24.99
00660115	Al Di Meola – Friday Night in San Francisco	$24.99
00125617	Best of Herb Ellis	$19.99
00699306	Jim Hall – Exploring Jazz Guitar	$19.99
00672353	The Joe Pass Collection	$22.99
00673216	John Patitucci	$22.99
00672374	Johnny Smith – Guitar Solos	$24.99

PIANO & KEYBOARD

00672487	Monty Alexander Plays Standards	$19.95
00672520	Count Basie Collection	$19.95
00192307	Bebop Piano Legends	$19.99
00113680	Blues Piano Legends	$22.99
00672526	The Bill Charlap Collection	$19.99
00278003	A Charlie Brown Christmas	$19.99
00672300	Chick Corea – Paint the World	$19.99
00146105	Bill Evans – Alone	$21.99
00672548	The Mastery of Bill Evans	$16.99
00672365	Bill Evans – Play Standards	$22.99
00121885	Bill Evans – Time Remembered	$22.99
00672510	Bill Evans Trio Vol. 1: 1959-1961	$29.99
00672511	Bill Evans Trio Vol. 2: 1962-1965	$27.99
00672512	Bill Evans Trio Vol. 3: 1968-1974	$29.99
00672513	Bill Evans Trio Vol. 4: 1979-1980	$24.95
00193332	Erroll Garner – Concert by the Sea	$22.99
00672486	Vince Guaraldi Collection	$19.99
00289644	The Definitive Vince Guaraldi	$39.99
00672419	Herbie Hancock Collection	$22.99
00672438	Hampton Hawes Collection	$19.95
00672322	Ahmad Jamal Collection	$27.99
00255671	Jazz Piano Masterpieces	$22.99
00124367	Jazz Piano Masters Play Rodgers & Hammerstein	$19.99
00672564	Best of Jeff Lorber	$19.99

00672476	Brad Mehldau Collection	$24.99
00672388	Best of Thelonious Monk	$22.99
00672389	Thelonious Monk Collection	$24.99
00672390	Thelonious Monk Plays Jazz Standards – Volume 1	$24.99
00672391	Thelonious Monk Plays Jazz Standards – Volume 2	$24.99
00672433	Jelly Roll Morton – The Piano Rolls	$19.99
00264094	Oscar Peterson – Night Train	$19.99
00672544	Oscar Peterson – Originals	$15.99
00672531	Oscar Peterson – Plays Duke Ellington	$27.99
00672563	Oscar Peterson – A Royal Wedding Suite	$19.99
00672569	Oscar Peterson – Tracks	$19.99
00672533	Oscar Peterson – Trios	$39.99
00672534	Very Best of Oscar Peterson	$27.99
00672371	Bud Powell Classics	$22.99
00672376	Bud Powell Collection	$24.99
00672507	Gonzalo Rubalcaba Collection	$19.95
00672303	Horace Silver Collection	$24.99
00672316	Art Tatum Collection	$27.99
00672355	Art Tatum Solo Book	$22.99
00672357	The Billy Taylor Collection	$24.95
00673215	McCoy Tyner	$22.99
00672321	Cedar Walton Collection	$19.95
00672519	Kenny Werner Collection	$19.95

SAXOPHONE

00672566	The Mindi Abair Collection	$14.99
00673244	Julian "Cannonball" Adderley Collection	$22.99
00673237	Michael Brecker	$24.99
00672429	Michael Brecker Collection	$24.99
00672529	John Coltrane – Giant Steps	$22.99
00672494	John Coltrane – A Love Supreme	$17.99
00672493	John Coltrane Plays "Coltrane Changes"	$19.95
00672453	John Coltrane Plays Standards	$24.99
00673233	John Coltrane Solos	$29.99
00672328	Paul Desmond Collection	$22.99
00672530	Kenny Garrett Collection	$24.99
00699375	Stan Getz	$19.99
00672377	Stan Getz – Bossa Novas	$24.99
00673254	Great Tenor Sax Solos	$22.99

00672523	Coleman Hawkins Collection	$24.99
00672330	Best of Joe Henderson	$24.99
00673239	Best of Kenny G	$22.99
00673229	Kenny G – Breathless	$19.99
00672462	Kenny G – Classics in the Key of G	$24.99
00672485	Kenny G – Faith: A Holiday Album	$17.99
00672373	Kenny G – The Moment	$22.99
00672498	Jackie McLean Collection	$19.95
00672372	James Moody Collection – Sax and Flute	$19.95
00672539	Gerry Mulligan Collection	$24.99
00102751	Sonny Rollins, Art Blakey & Kenny Drew with the Modern Jazz Quartet	$17.99
00675000	David Sanborn Collection	$19.95
00672491	The New Best of Wayne Shorter	$24.99
00672550	The Sonny Stitt Collection	$19.95
00672524	Lester Young Collection	$22.99

TROMBONE

00672332	J.J. Johnson Collection	$24.99
00672489	Steve Turré Collection	$19.99

TRUMPET

00672557	Herb Alpert Collection	$19.99
00672480	Louis Armstrong Collection	$19.99
00672481	Louis Armstrong Plays Standards	$19.99
00672435	Chet Baker Collection	$24.99
00672556	Best of Chris Botti	$19.99
00672448	Miles Davis – Originals, Vol. 1	$19.99
00672451	Miles Davis – Originals, Vol. 2	$19.95
00672449	Miles Davis – Standards, Vol. 2	$19.95
00672479	Dizzy Gillespie Collection	$19.95
00673214	Freddie Hubbard	$19.99
00672506	Chuck Mangione Collection	$22.99
00672525	Arturo Sandoval – Trumpet Evolution	$19.99

HAL•LEONARD®

Visit our web site for songlists or to order online from your favorite music retailer at
www.halleonard.com